Human Habitats

LIFE IN THE

MOUNTAINS

By Holly Duhig

BookLife
PUBLISHING

©2019
BookLife Publishing Ltd.
King's Lynn
Norfolk PE30 4LS

ISBN: 978-1-78637-589-6

Written by:
Holly Duhig

Edited by:
Emilie Dufresne

Designed by:
Jasmine Pointer

CONTENTS

Words that look like this can be found in the glossary on page 24.

HUMAN HABITATS

Can you spot the owl in this tree?

A habitat is a place that provides a living thing with food, water and shelter. An animal's body needs to be **adapted** to its habitat. For example, owls have feathers that **camouflage** them against trees.

Humans also have habitats. Unlike most animals, humans can survive in many different habitats and our bodies don't need to be adapted to them. Some human habitats are pretty extreme!

We humans can't camouflage ourselves, but we can make camouflage clothing!

MOUNTAIN HABITATS

Many countries have mountains and mountain ranges. Some mountains are home to cities, while others are home to villages and towns where people live and work. Mountains are often home to **nomadic tribes**.

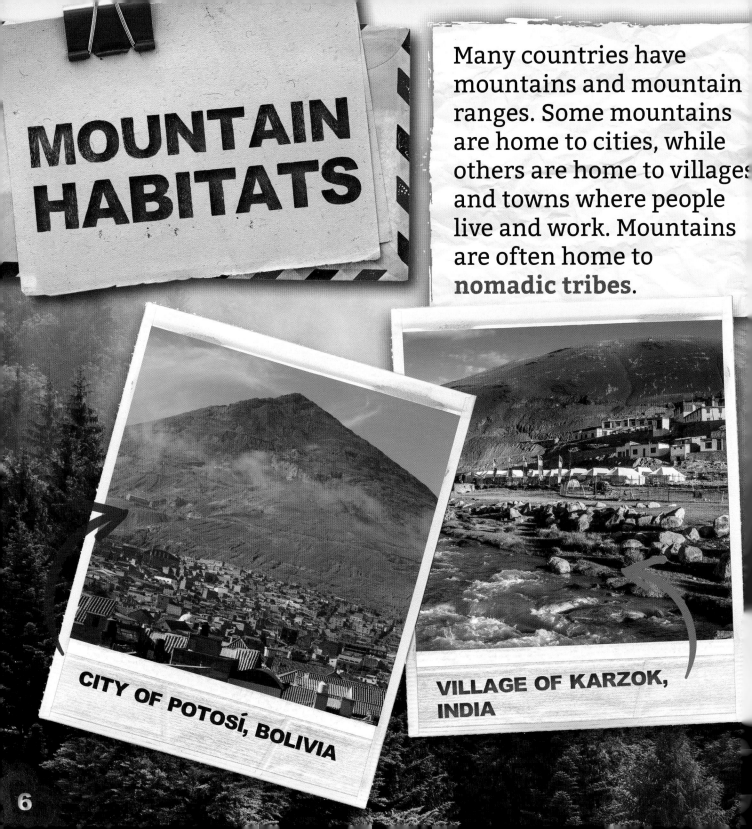

CITY OF POTOSÍ, BOLIVIA

VILLAGE OF KARZOK, INDIA

Mountains can make for extreme human habitats.

Mountains are great places for extreme sports such as skiing and rock climbing. However, with the high **altitudes**, rock falls and extreme temperatures, mountains can be very dangerous.

LIFE IN THE
TIEN SHAN MOUNTAINS

KYRGYZ NATIONAL CLOTHING

Kyrgyz (say: keer-gis) people are from the country Kyrgyzstan (say: keer-gis-stan). Many Kyrgyz people live nomadic lives high up in the Tien Shan mountain range. Nomadic means having no fixed home.

These Kyrgyz people travel to higher land in the warm summer months to find new land for their **livestock**. During winter, when it gets too cold to live at such high altitudes, they travel back down to their villages.

At night, temperatures in the mountains can drop well below freezing.

YURTS

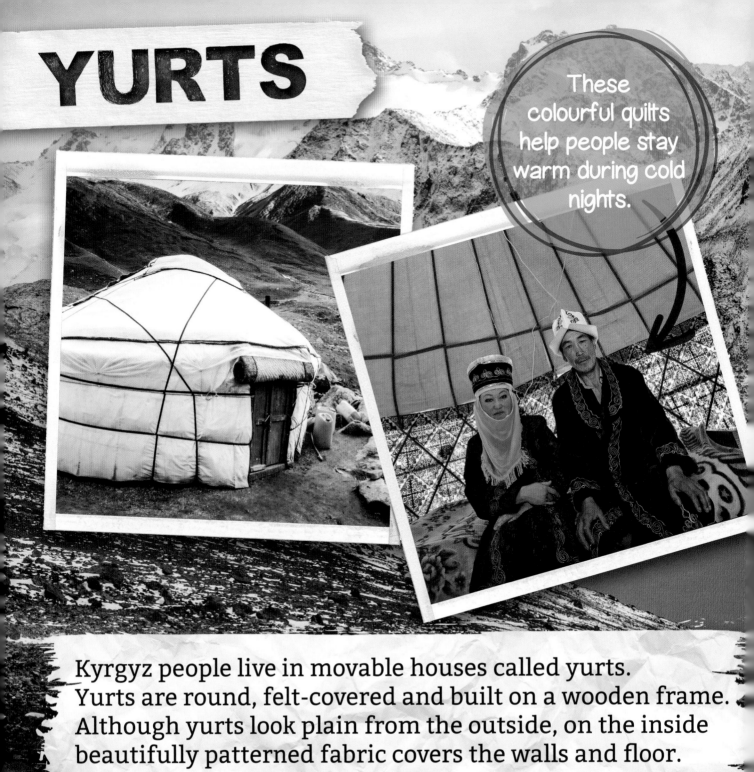

These colourful quilts help people stay warm during cold nights.

Kyrgyz people live in movable houses called yurts. Yurts are round, felt-covered and built on a wooden frame. Although yurts look plain from the outside, on the inside beautifully patterned fabric covers the walls and floor.

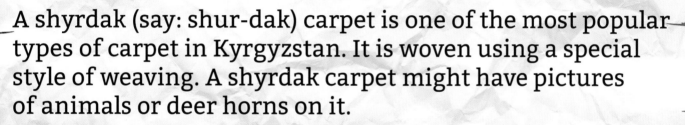

A shyrdak (say: shur-dak) carpet is one of the most popular types of carpet in Kyrgyzstan. It is woven using a special style of weaving. A shyrdak carpet might have pictures of animals or deer horns on it.

Different patterns have different meanings.

LIFE IN THE HIMALAYAS

MOUNT EVEREST

The Himalayas are a mountain range in Asia that run through a region called Tibet. They are home to the Earth's highest mountain, Mount Everest, which is around 8,848 metres tall!

High up in the mountains there is less oxygen in the air than there is closer to **sea level**. Tibetan people's bodies have adapted to the lack of oxygen so they find it easier to breathe the thin mountain air.

Oxygen is the gas that humans and animals need to breathe to stay alive.

MONASTERIES IN TIBET

The main religion in Tibet is Buddhism and there are many Buddhist monasteries in the mountains. A monastery is a building where people, such as monks and nuns, live and **worship**.

BUDDHIST NUN

BUDDHIST MONK

RONGBUK MONASTERY

Rongbuk Monastery is the highest monastery in the world. It is around 5,000 metres above sea level and is on the north face of Mount Everest. Many people take **pilgrimages** to Rongbuk Monastery.

LIFE IN THE ANDES MOUNTAINS

El Alto is Spanish for 'The Heights'.

The city of El Alto can be found in the mountains of Bolivia. It sits at around 4,150 metres above sea level on the edge of a big **canyon**.

People who visit El Alto might get altitude sickness because there is less oxygen in the mountain air. Altitude sickness happens when a person's body can't get enough oxygen, which causes people to feel sick, dizzy and out of breath.

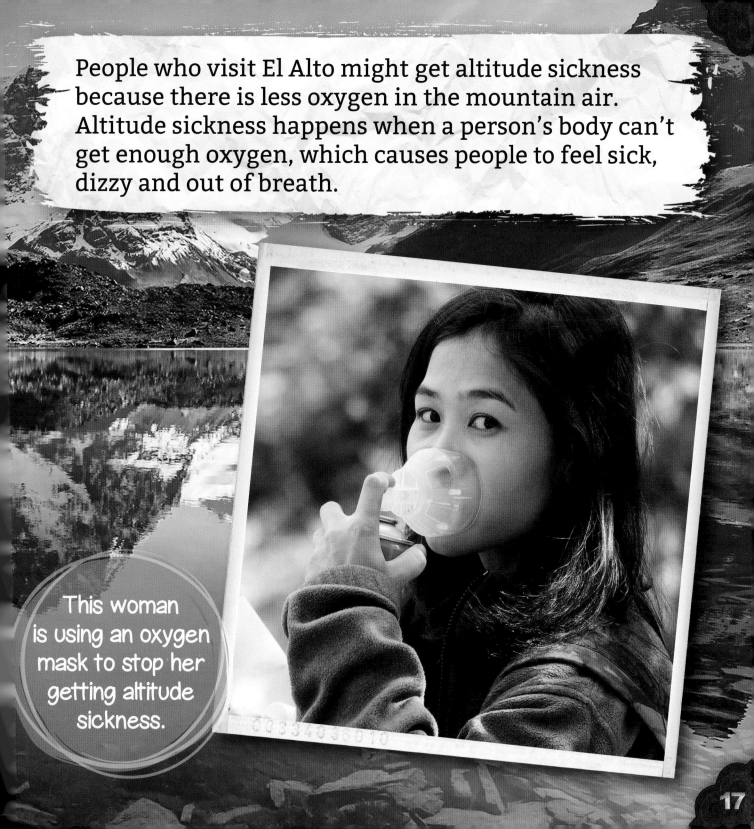

This woman is using an oxygen mask to stop her getting altitude sickness.

GETTING AROUND EL ALTO

CABLE CAR

In El Alto, the easiest way to get up the mountain is in a cable car. Tall towers and cables hang the cars high in the air, and pull them up the mountainside.

El Alto's cable cars run partly using solar energy.

Most people use the cable car system to get to El Alto from the nearby city of La Paz. Cable cars are less harmful to the environment than buses and cars.

ANCIENT LIFE IN THE ANDES MOUNTAINS

The Incas were part of an **ancient civilisation** who lived in the Andes mountains thousands of years ago. Just like people living in El Alto in the present day, the Incas also had to deal with the thin air and cold nights in the Andes.

MACHU PICCHU

TERRACES

Machu Picchu was an ancient Incan city. Unlike the people living in El Alto, there were no cable cars to get around. The Incas had very different ways of getting to their city.

The Incas made a road to Machu Picchu by cutting a path into a cliff. Part of the path was missing and was covered by a plank of wood that could be taken away to stop people getting to the city!

The ruins of Machu Picchu are around 2,430 metres above sea level.

ACTIVITY

Make sure to take a tent and sleeping bag for the cold nights!

If you had to survive a night in the mountains, what things would you pack in your rucksack?

GLOSSARY

ADAPTED	changed over time to suit the environment
ALTITUDES	the heights of locations in relation to sea level or ground level
ANCIENT CIVILISATION	a early society that became the basis for later societies
CAMOUFLAGE	traits that allow an animal to hide itself in a habitat
CANYON	a large valley with steep sides
LIVESTOCK	animals that are kept for farming purposes
NOMADIC TRIBES	communities of people who do not live in one place
PILGRIMAGES	religious journeys or treks, usually to a specific place or building
SEA LEVEL	the level of the sea's surface
SOLAR ENERGY	energy from the Sun
WORSHIP	a religious act where a person expresses their love for a god

INDEX